Arcola Theatre in association with
Nick of Time Productions and Jemir

Drones, Ba
Drones

ʊɔıd
ɔatre

This Tuesday

Text **Ron Hutchinson
& Christina Lamb**

Direction **Nicolas Kent**

The Kid

Text **Da⸱ ⸱ Greig**

Direction **Mehmet Ergen**

and

Verbatim material from an interview with **Clive Stafford-Smith**

Cast **Anne Adams
Joseph Balderrama
Sam Dale
Raj Ghatak
Tom McKay
Rose Reynolds**

Design	**Lucy Sierra**
Lighting and Video Design	**Richard Williamson**
Sound Design	**Neil McKeown**
Production Manager	**Ben Karakashian**
Stage Manager	**Sarah Julie Pujol**
Casting	**Marilyn Johnson**
Production Electrician	**Josh Hale**
Costume Supervisor	**Hanne Talbot**
Literary Consultant	**Jack Bradley**
Public Relations	**Kevin Wilson**
Volunteer ASM	**Rafe Gibbons**

First performed Wednesday 2 November 2016
at Arcola Theatre, London

These plays were commissioned from an original idea by Nicolas Kent (for Nick
of Time Productic   dation

Special thaı

Anne Adams
Maxine & Shauna

London theatre includes: *Burning Bridges* (Theatre 503). **Chicago theatre includes:** *The Old Masters, Cherry Orchard* (Steppenwolf Theatre Company); *Mauritius* (Northlight Theatre); *Orange Lemon Egg Canary* (Uma Productions); *This Is Our Youth, Life and Limb, Imagining Brad* (Pine Box Theatre). Anne can be seen in Braden LuBell's web series *Quick & Dirty*, as well as upcoming feature films *Samuel Street* directed by Aliakbar Campwala and *55 Steps* directed by Bille August. Also a writer, her play *Strange Country* was the inaugural recipient of New Light Theater Project's New Light New Voices Award, and was produced this past July in NYC.

Joseph Balderamma
Jay & Ramon

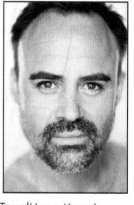

Joseph trained at LAMDA, was a member of NYT and studied History at the University of Glasgow. **Theatre includes**: *Labyrinth* (Hampstead); *The White House Murder Case* (Orange Tree); *The Miser* (Royal Exchange); *Wet Weather Cover* (King's Head/West End); *No Such Cold Thing* (Tricycle); *The Accidental Death of an Anarchist* (Colchester); *Hamlet, Arabian Nights, The Merchant of Venice* (Creation), *Cinderella is Not Enough, Biloxi Blues* (CPP), *Romeo and Juliet* (ETT Tour/Hong Kong). **Television includes**: *Benidorm; Capital; I Live With Models; Not Going Out; The Armada: 12 Days To Save England; Borgia; Episodes; Schizo Samurai Shitzu; Canoe Man; Holby City; Bremner, Bird and Fortune; The Omid Djalili Show; The Bill; The Vice; The Robinsons.* **Film includes**: *Tad Jones: The Hero Returns; Spectre; Meet The Firm: Revenge In Rio; Jack and Jill; The Nutcracker: The Untold Story.* **Radio includes**: *The Clinton's, Prayers For The Stolen, The Weapon, The Old Man and The Sea; We Are Water* (BBC). As a regular voice artist, Joseph has recorded numerous voice overs, commercials and audio books and is the voice of regular character Cotter in the video game version of *Game of Thrones*.

Sam Dale
General Ben Crow
& Clive Stafford-Smith

Sam trained at Central School of Speech & Drama. **Theatre includes:** *Comedians* (Wyndham's/UK tour); *Dancing at Lughnasa* (Garrick/UK & Ireland tour); *A Handful of Dust for Shared Experience* (Lyric/Riverside/UK tour); *Gaslight* (Theatr Clwyd); *The Possessed* (Almeida/ Théâtre de L'Europe); *Julius Caesar* (Birmingham Rep); *Hamlet* (AFTLS US tour); *The Beaux' Stratagem* (Stephen Joseph Theatre, Scarborough); *Says I Says He* (Sheffield Crucible/Mickery Theatre, Amsterdam).
Television includes: *Chips With Everything; Rock Follies* (Series 2); *Harry's Game; Catchpenny Twist; The Government Inspector; All Creatures Great and Small.*
Film includes: *Brothers and Sisters; Animal Shadows.*
Radio includes: Sam has done a multitude of radio dramas, readings and live broadcasts, both for the BBC and for various independent companies. He has been a member of the BBC Radio Drama Company on three occasions.

Raj Ghatak
Captain Mario Garcia

Theatre includes: *Hector* (ATG); *The Low Road, The Spiral, Free Outgoing, Shades/ Unheard Voices* (Royal Court); *The Bad, Sad and Broken Hearted, Soho Cinders* (Soho Theatre); *Golgotha* (Conspirators Kitchen/Tristan Bates); *Bombay Dreams* (West End); *The Great Extension, High Heel Parrotfish and Airport 2000* (Theatre Royal Stratford East). **Television includes:** *Eastenders; Taboo; Dead Set; The 7.39; Sinchronicity.* **Film includes:** *Mrs Brown's Boys D'Movie; Starter for 10; Defrosted; Diary of a Thagee.*

Tom McKay
Doug & Pete

Tom trained at LAMDA. **Theatre includes:** *Dedication* (Nuffield); *Julius Caesar* (The Globe); *The Great Game* (Tricycle/US tour/Public Theatre NYC); *Greta Garbo Came to Donegal* (Tricycle); *Frost Nixon* (Donmar Warehouse/West End); *Rough Cuts* (Royal Court); *On The Third Day* (West End); *Gladiator Games* (Sheffield Crucible/Theatre Royal Stratford East); *Macbeth* (Almeida); *The Arab Israeli Cookbook* (Gate); *Romeo & Juliet* (Theatre Royal Bath); *Henry V* (National Theatre); *Simplicity* (Orange Tree); *Elizabeth Rex* (Birmingham Rep); *Mother Clap's Molly House* (Aldwych Theatre/National Theatre); *Macbeth, Lord of the Flies* (RSC). **Film includes:** *The Harrow; Kill Command; Wrong Turn 3; Clubbed; The Feral Generation; Imagine Me & You; Chromophobia.*

Rose Reynolds
Meredith & Alice

Rose trained at Guildhall. **Theatre includes:** *My Children! My Africa!* (Tristan Bates/Trafalgar Studios); *Twelfth Night* (Sheffield Crucible/ETT); *Titus Andronicus, Mad World My Masters, Candice* (RSC); *Tiger Tail* (Nuffield). **Film includes:** *The World's End; Drunk Dialling* (short film); *On The Edge* (short film). **Television includes:** *Crackanory Series 4; Wasted; Poldark 2; Hastings Music Festival; Doctors; Our Zoo.*

Mehmet Ergen
Director, *The Kid*

Mehmet has been Artistic Director of Arcola Theatre since founding it in 2000. Previously he was Artistic Director of the Southwark Playhouse (which he co-founded) from 1993 to 1999, and Associate Producer at BAC. Mehmet is also Artistic Director of Arcola Istanbul (Talimhane Theatre), which he founded in 2008. He has won a variety of awards for his work including: the Time Out Award for Outstanding Achievement, a Time Out Award for Best Fringe Production, the Angela Carter Award, the Peter Brook Empty Space Award and the WhatsOnStage Award for Best New Musical. His productions at the Arcola include *Clarion, Enemy of the People, Cradle Will Rock, Shrapnel: 34 Fragments of a Massacre, Don Gil of the Green Breeches, Mare Rider, Sweet Smell of Success* and *The Painter*. Other work includes *Bastard of Istanbul, After Miss Julie, It Felt Empty..., Pillowman, King Lear, Macbeth, Fool for Love, Betrayal, Ashes to Ashes, Water's Edge, Dumb Show, Lost in the Stars, In the Jungle of the Cities, Piano - after Platonov*. His work has been seen in Netherlands, Germany, Turkey, Sweden, Cyprus and Canada. He has just finished filming *Inferno*, appearing with Tom Hanks.

Nicolas Kent
Director, *This Tuesday*

Nicolas Kent was Artistic Director of the Tricycle Theatre, London, from 1984 to 2012. He has directed productions at over 100 theatres around the world including the West End, New York, the National Theatre, RSC, Royal Court, Donmar Warehouse, Hampstead Theatre, Lyric Hammersmith and Young Vic. He is known for his political pieces at the Tricycle, where the verbatim plays he directed became known as the Tricycle Tribunal plays. *Half the Picture, The Colour of Justice* (The Stephen Lawrence Inquiry), *Nuremberg, Srebrenica* and *Bloody Sunday* (Olivier Award for Special Achievement) were all broadcast by the BBC, and two were performed in the Houses of Parliament and on Capitol Hill. In 2009, he directed the 9-hour trilogy *The Great Game - Afghanistan* (nominated for an Olivier) in London, which subsequently toured the USA, and had two command performances for the Pentagon in Washington in 2011. He collaborated with Gillian Slovo on *Guantanamo* (2004) and *The Riots* (2012) and most recently on *Another World* which he directed this year at the National Theatre. He directed *The Nightmares of Carlos Fuentes* at Arcola in 2014.

David Greig
Writer, *The Kid*

David is currently under commission to write new plays for the Royal Court and the National Theatre of Scotland and is developing an original television series with co-creators David Harrower and John Crowley for Sister Pictures. He became Artistic Director of the Royal Lyceum Theatre in Edinburgh in 2016. **Theatre includes:** *The Suppliant Women* (Actors Touring Company/Lyceum); *The Lorax* (Old Vic); *Lanark* (The Lyceum, Edinburgh International Festival); *Charlie and the Chocolate Factory* (West End/Broadway (2017)); *The Events* (Actors Touring Company/ Young Vic/Brageteatret & Schauspielhaus Wien); *The Strange Undoing of Prudencia Hart* (NTS at Tron Theatre/Royal Court/Welsh Centre/CLF Theatre/UK tour); *Fragile / Cello* (Young Vic/Southwark Playhouse/ Latitude Festival); *Dunsinane* (Hampstead Theatre/UK Tour); *Midsummer* (Traverse/ Soho Theatre/Tricycle/ International tour); *Miniskirts of Kabul* (Tricycle); *Damascus* (Traverse/Tricycle); *Being Norwegian* (Shunt Vaults); *The American Pilot* (The Other Place/Soho Theatre/ Manhattan Theatre Club).

Christina Lamb
Writer, *This Tuesday*

Christina Lamb is one of Britain's leading foreign correspondents and a bestselling author. She has reported from most of the world's hotspots but her particular passions are Afghanistan and Pakistan which she has covered since an unexpected wedding invitation led her to Karachi in 1987 when she was just 21. Within two years she had been named Young Journalist of the Year. Since then she has won numerous awards including five times being named Foreign Correspondent of the Year and Europe's top war reporting prize, the Prix Bayeux. She was made an OBE in 2013. Last year she won Amnesty International's Newspaper Journalist of the Year for reporting from inside Libyan detention centres. Currently Chief Foreign Correspondent for the Sunday Times of London, her postings have included South Africa, Pakistan, Brazil and Washington and she has recently reported on the refugee crisis across Europe and camps for women enslaved by Boko Haram in Nigeria and ISIS in Iraq. She has written eight books including the bestselling *The Africa House* and *I Am Malala* and is a patron of Afghan Connection and on the board of the Institute of

War and Peace Reporting. Her latest books are *Farewell Kabul; From Afghanistan to a More Dangerous World* and *Nujeen; One Girl's Incredible Journey from War-torn Syria in a Wheelchair.*

Ron Hutchinson
Writer, *This Tuesday*

Ron Hutchinson was Writer in Residence at the Royal Shakespeare Company and has had plays performed at the National Theatre, the Royal Court Theatre, the Goodman, the Public Theatre, the Mark Taper Forum and The Old Globe. Other stage plays include *Moonlight and Magnolias*, *The Hook* (adapted from Arthur Miller's screenplay), *Says I Says He*, and *Rat In The Skull*, and adaptations of Mikhail Bulgakov's *Flight*, and *The Master and Margarita*, and Carl Zuckmayer's *The Captain of Kopenick*. In 2014 he directed his play about Tango, *Flying Into Daylight*, in its premier production. Its first foreign language production will be in Prague in 2017. Ron is a winner of the John Whiting Award and other awards including the Dramatist's Circle Award. He is an Emmy winning feature and television writer whose credits include *Murderers Among Us, The Simon Wiesenthal Story, The Josephine Baker Story, The Burning Season, The Ten Commandments* and *Traffic; the miniseries.* Currently his six-part series based on corruption in the pharmaceutical industry is shooting in Dublin and Montreal. He lives and works in New York and has taught screenwriting at the American Film Institute in Los Angeles, and has recently returned to writing radio plays.

Lucy Sierra
Design

Recent credits include: *Cathy* (Cardboard Citizens Tour); *The Grand Journey* (Bombay Sapphire Immersive Experience); *The Tempest* (Royal & Derngate); *Giving* (Hampstead); *Another World: Losing Our Children to Islamic State* (Shed, National Theatre); *Calculating Kindness* (Camden People's Theatre); *Snow White & Rose Red* (Rash Dash/Cambridge Arts Theatre); *Abyss* (Arcola); *Benefit, We Are All Misfits* (Cardboard Citizens Tour); *We Have Fallen* (Underbelly); *If You Don't Let Us Dream, We Won't Let You Sleep* (Royal Court); *Sign of The Times* (Theatre Royal Bury); *The Bear* (Improbable Tour); *Sweeney Todd, David Copperfield, White Nights* (Octagon Bolton); *Symmetry* (Southwark Playhouse); *Songs Inside* (Gate); *Fewer Emergencies* (Oxford Playhouse). As Associate Designer: National Theatre, Royal Court, Young Vic.

Richard Williamson
Lighting and Video Design

Richard trained at LAMDA. Previous work includes: *Richard III, An Arab Tragedy* (Swan Theatre Stratford/International tour); *Jason and the Argonauts, Septimus Bean and His Amazing Machine* (Unicorn); *Shrapnel* (also video), *Mare Rider, Boy With a Suitcase, Peer Gynt, Macbeth, A Midsummer Night's Dream, The Night Just Before the Forest, Tartuffe, Through a Cloud, King Arthur, Mojo Mickybo, The Great Theatre of the World, Tombstone Tales, The Country* (Arcola Theatre); *The Body* (Barbican); *The Easter Rising and Thereafter* (Jermyn Street); *Rotterdam* (Theatre 503/Trafalgar Studios); *The Dark Side of Love* (Roundhouse); *In My Name, Boris World King* (Trafalgar Studios); *Amphibians* (Bridewell); *Thrill Me* (Tristan Bates/Charing Cross Theatre/UK tour); *The Last Session* (Tristan Bates); *Twentieth Century Boy* (New Wolsey Ipswich); *Re:Home* (also video), *Brenda* (The Yard); *Play Size* (Young Vic); *The Al-Hamlet Summit* (Tokyo International Festival/International tour); *Strangers In Between, Ballo, Tosco, Denial, Someone To Blame* (King's Head Theatre); *Summer Begins* (Southwark Playhouse). Richard is Head of Production for C venues Edinburgh, and is a Trustee of the King's Head Theatre.

Neil McKeown
Sound Design

Neil has been producing music for over 20 years, recently concentrating on sound design and composition for theatre. Since moving his focus he has worked on a wide variety of shows, with Shrapnel being nominated for Best Sound Design in the 2015 Offies. Other credits include: *The Local Stigmatic* (Old Red Lion); *Richard II, Children of War, Clarion, Shrapnel, The Revenger's Tragedy, Mahmud ile Yezida, Between Us, The Intruder and The Bald Prima Dona* (Arcola); *The Bacchae, Richard III, Say your name* (Blue Elephant); *The Women* (GSA); *The Caucasian Chalk Circle, The Merchant of Venice* (Brockley Jack); *Tamburlaine, Troilus & Cressida, Coriolanus* (Tristan Bates); *His Dark Materials* (Nuffield, Southampton); *Henry V, Closer to Heaven* (Union); *The Water's Edge* (Talimhane, Istanbul); *Dead in the Water* (Brighton Fringe); *Shang-a-Lang* (King's Head); *The Door* (Park Theatre).

Ben Karakashian
Production Manager

Ben graduated from Royal Holloway University of London with a BA Honors in Drama and Theatre Studies. Production management credits include: *Acedian Pirates* (Theatre 503);

Ragtime (Charing Cross Theatre); *Frontier Trilogy* (Rabenhof Theatre/Vienna); *Home Chat* (Finborough Theatre);*Titanic the Musical, In the Bar of a Tokyo Hotel, The Mikado* (Charing Cross Theatre); *Kenny Morgan, The Divided Laing* (Arcola Theatre); *The Frontier Trilogy* (Edinburgh Fringe Festival); *Contact.com, The Man Who Shot Liberty Valance* (Park Theatre); Our Ajax (Southwark Playhouse); *The Bunker Trilogy* (Southwark Playhouse/Seoul Performing Arts Festival/ Stratford Circus).

Sarah Julie Pujol
Stage Manager

Sarah Julie is a freelance Stage Manager based in London. Recent credits include *Kenny Morgan, Creative Engagement Winter Season, The Dog, The Night and the Knife* (Arcola); *Sprung!* (Kazzum); *Rice Paper Tales* (Trikhon); *A Christmas Carol The Musical* (Castle); *Roaring Trade* (Park); *A Strange Wild Song* (UK Tour); *64 Squares* (UK Tour); *The Secret Diary of Adrian Mole Aged 13 and 3/4 The Musical,* Abigail's Party (Curve Theatre); *Yeh-Shen* (Albany); *The Unnatural Tragedy* (Ovalhouse); *The Flying Roast Goose* (Blue Elephant); *Foreplay* (King's Head Theatre); *The Husbands* (Soho Theatre/UK Tour); *Talkback Festival* (Tristan Bates); *XY* (Theatre503); *The Old Woman* (Palace/EU Tour).

Hanne Talbot
Costume Supervisor

Hanne trained at the Royal Central School of Speech & Drama. Credits as Costume Supervisor include: *Kenny Morgan* revival (Arcola); *Decades* (Ovalhouse); *A Flea In Her Ear* (Tabard Theatre); *Othello* (Smooth Faced Gentlemen). As Wardrobe Mistress: *All or Nothing: The Mod Musical* (The Vaults Theatre); *Pentecost* (Derby Live). Hanne has assisted on productions including: *Funny Girl* (Menier Chocolate Factory); *Sunny Afternoon* (Harold Pinter Theatre); *Sleeping Beauty* (Matthew Bourne's New Adventures); *Wonderland* (Hampstead).

Jemima Khan
Co-producer

Jemima recently set up Instinct Productions, to produce quality documentaries, drama and film. Her background is in journalism; as associate editor of *The New Statesman* and European editor-at-large for *Vanity Fair*. Khan was also the executive producer for the BAFTA nominated documentary film *We Steal Secrets: The Story of Wikileaks* by Alex Gibney and the executive producer for the documentary films, *Unmanned: America's Drone Wars* and *Making A Killing: Guns, Greed and the NRA.*

Arcola Theatre is one of London's leading off-West End theatres.

Locally engaged and internationally minded, Arcola stages a diverse programme of plays, operas and musicals. World-class productions from major artists appear alongside cutting-edge work from the most exciting emerging companies.

Arcola delivers one of London's most extensive community engagement programmes, creating over 5000 opportunities every year. By providing research and development space to diverse artists, Arcola champions theatre that's more engaging and representative. Its pioneering environmental initiatives are internationally renowned, and aim to make Arcola the world's first carbon-neutral theatre.

www.arcolatheatre.com
020 7503 1646

DRONES, BABY, DRONES

DRONES, BABY, DRONES

This Tuesday
by Ron Hutchinson and Christina Lamb

The Kid
by David Greig

OBERON BOOKS
LONDON

WWW.OBERONBOOKS.COM

This collection first published in 2016 by Oberon Books Ltd
521 Caledonian Road, London N7 9RH
Tel: +44 (0) 20 7607 3637 / Fax: +44 (0) 20 7607 3629
e-mail: info@oberonbooks.com
www.oberonbooks.com

A catalogue record for this book is available from the British
Library.

PB ISBN: 9781786820785
E ISBN: 9781786820792

Printed and bound by 4edge Limited, Essex, UK.

Contents

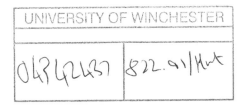

THIS TUESDAY

Characters

MAXINE

JAY

DOUG

MEREDITH

BEN

MARIO

In the BLACKOUT we hear screeching tires and the sound of metal hitting metal as two cars collide at high speed, followed by the impact of a third car. In the noise of colliding steel and shattering of glass we see the red line of a heart-rate monitor, showing a weak, irregular beat.

THE LIGHTS RISE on MAXINE FORMAN on a mobile as she paces –

MAXINE: – on Virginia Avenue, just outside the Watergate at two in the morning. The cops think she was doing sixty, seventy. It's a mess, a real fucking mess and I want to go in there and take a baseball bat to her but I really just want to hug her and say it's okay baby, Mom's here, everything is okay as long as you walk out of here –

She squeezes her forehead –

I'm fine, I'm fine, it doesn't matter what I'm feeling, this is about her but the thing is I need somebody to cover me here, in case the doctors have anything to tell me or I have, you know, a decision to make –

As she listens, she looks at the heart rate –

That decision, maybe, you know which one? The donor thing.

(Listens.)

Yes, that's how serious it is – that's what I could be looking at here and I need to get my head into a place where I can make that decision if that's what has to be done and it's five a.m. and there's a real problem because I have to be somewhere now for an hour, at least –

(Listens.)

A meeting, it's something I have to be in for every Tuesday, it's important, really really important –

(Listens.)

Nothing is more important than my daughter, I know but you can't keep your life in neat little boxes so could I ask you to get over here to George Washington so somebody is around from the family to be told any news because they put her into a coma after the emergency operation when they tried to stop the bleeding, check the internal damage –

She takes a deep breath, looks as if she's about to lose it –

You should have seen her, Sis. A head-on crash. She wasn't wearing a seat belt – the number of times I told her, drilled it into her – and the airbag – oh Jesus – oh Christ – oh God – it blew her right out of the car – the door lock burst and when that – that fucking *thing* went off it knocked her fifteen feet across the street and she was hit – Brittany never did anything by halves – another car hit her so all along one side – as well as the cuts and whatever's broken and whatever is wrong inside – her skin – poor kid – poor poor kid – when she got dragged along the street –

Another deep breath, forcing herself to calm down –

Let's just say it's going to be a couple months before she's in that bikini again, flashing what she's got for that worthless boyfriend of hers who – wouldn't you know it – walked away without a scratch –

She turns as JAY NEROLI appears with two coffees –

I gotta go. I'm asking for a big one. Now you get a chance to play big sister instead of me –

She closes the phone.

JAY: Made a couple of calls. The cops. Lawyer friend of mine who specializes in DUI. This is what it's going to be, right? She was high on something?

MAXINE: What else?

JAY: They find anything in the car, do you know?

MAXINE: I don't know that.

JAY: But they will?

MAXINE: She's out of control, Jay. I thought I could handle her but –

She gives a helpless shrug, indicates the coffees –

One of those for me?

JAY: Vending machine. Going to taste like shit.

MAXINE: This time of day what doesn't?

She sips it, makes a face, checks that no one can overhear –

Today –

Abdullah al-Rizvi is Number Three in the Haqqani network. I've been trying to nail him for years. We know where he's going to be in the next few hours; at a village belonging to the Araki clan in Waziristan. We have ground coordinates for him. This is human intel as well as satellite imagery. We have actual eyeballs on him.

At today's circle jerk in the White House Situation Room in an hour I need you guys in Legal to help me make the case that we kill him –

THE LIGHTS SNAP OUT ON THEM and RISE on the thirty year old DOUG GIBSON, trying to get dressed with as little noise as possible. A yawning MEREDITH ZANE, a twenty-something intern heads towards him, in briefs and T-shirt.

MEREDITH: Sneaking out on me?

DOUG: Didn't want to wake you. Go back to bed.

MEREDITH: Got to get back to my boyfriend's place. Oh, that's right. You are my boyfriend. You have to get back to your wife.

DOUG: You know I have that thing this morning.

MEREDITH: What are we going to do if they change the day of the week you do that thing? The thing you do early Tuesdays? You'd have to come up with another reason to spend Monday nights here.

Before he can answer –

7

MEREDITH: How's your hand?

DOUG: Fine.

He flexes his knuckles, tests his right hand.

MEREDITH: Didn't sleep much. There was an accident down there. Outside the building.

DOUG: Accident?

MEREDITH: Somebody hit another car head on and then ploughed into a lighting pole before another car hit them both. There were cops, paramedics, flashing lights. You slept through it.

DOUG: I guess.

He yawns.

MEREDITH: Come back to bed.

DOUG: Wish I could.

MEREDITH: Maybe they'll cancel your meeting today?

DOUG: They never cancel this one.

MEREDITH: Tell them you're sick.

DOUG: I have a job I like. I want to keep it.

MEREDITH: You want to keep me, too? Or am I just for Monday nights?

DOUG: We'll talk about this, okay? But not now. I need to keep my head clear. Any idea where my pants are?

She hands him his pants –

MEREDITH: Keep your little noodle clear because you're going to advise the President who he should kill today?

DOUG: That's – you don't know anything about what I do there.

MEREDITH: I'm not an idiot, Doug. There are no idiots at Swarthmore – unless they're on the faculty.

DOUG: You're very smart and very beautiful and this is very dangerous –

MEREDITH: I figured it out. How necessary to *national security* it is that you should be on top of your game. Isn't that what you tell Holly? Loyal, trusting Holly. In that nice little fake Colonial of yours out in the 'burbs? To justify being away Monday nights?

DOUG: Don't do this –

MEREDITH: Face it. You work for a guy who campaigned against water boarding and secret rendition, virtually accused the CIA of running torture factories but who ended up heading the world's first high tech assassination bureau –

DOUG: *(Automatically.)* Selective targeting option –

MEREDITH: – who commits what one day might be seen as a war crime in our names by playing Whack-a-Mole from thirty-five thousand feet on almost a daily basis –

DOUG: *(Automatically.)* Fulfilling his pledge to keep our young men and women out of harm's way –

MEREDITH: – and you need to be in the room too as a member of the – his – National Security team so of course you have to borrow your old college buddy's place in the Watergate Apartments Monday nights to get a good night's screwing your brains out – correction – to get a good night's sleep and the reason you need to be there? – oh yes – in case the President doesn't bend over when you tell him to.

DOUG: You nailed it. Whatever you say, whatever you want. I have to get out of here. My shirt?

She hands him his shirt –

MEREDITH: What's your part in that operation, Doug? When he pushes back against the name of a target? Are you the guy holding the tube of Vaseline? Or do you put him in the headlock while the others work on his rear end?

DOUG: Whatever you say. Can I have two minutes to clear my head?

MEREDITH: I figured it out last Tuesday, when we found a way to meet in the afternoon. You fucked me way, way better than anybody ever fucked me in my life. It was an erotic masterpiece. A symphony of lust. When I staggered out of the shower with my pussy still ringing like a bell you were on the edge of the bed, naked. I thought you were admiring your bruised and battered dick but you were flicking through the TV channels until you found what you were looking for – a report on the killing of a terrorist big shot. That's when Monday night and Tuesday morning fitted into place. So who's up this Tuesday? Who are you going to tell the President to strap on his six guns and go kill today?

He's stung –

DOUG: All targeting decisions in that program are arrived at on an individualized basis, after careful consideration and the weighing of input from multiple sources –

MEREDITH: – it says on the Warning Label. *Legal disclaimer. Standing under several pounds of high explosive travelling at you at the speed of sound can be dangerous to your health.*

DOUG: We're at war, Meredith. We didn't choose to be in one but we are.

MEREDITH: You're a decent guy. I couldn't have fallen in love with a monster, could I? I just don't get how a decent man can square this with his conscience, even in a war.

DOUG: There are people out there trying to kill us.

MEREDITH: And I guess fighting them remotely with drones is cheaper than catching them and having to give them three squares a day for life in Guantanamo?

DOUG: You're not a big fan of Gitmo either.

MEREDITH: Not if you're water-boarding them there in my name.

DOUG: *Government is force.* Know who said that? Our very first President. This present one has come to understand it and maybe that process has not come easily to him – I should know because I'm around him most days and that's it – we are not having this conversation.

MEREDITH: It would make it a lot simpler for you if we could make love remotely, too. Is there a drone for that yet? You could sit in that farmhouse style kitchen – that's how I imagine it, your kitchen – and keep chatting to Holly while you – you know?

He keeps dressing –

DOUG: Assuming the job of somebody like me was to advise him about the pros and cons of any one particular strike – the President should let a guy we have in our sights go free?

MEREDITH: Maybe.

DOUG: To kill or maim dozens of people? Two hundred? A thousand? Three thousand? Maybe more, this time?

MEREDITH: Maybe.

DOUG: On grounds of what?

MEREDITH: Morality. Decency. Humanity.

DOUG: Sure it's not taste? That it's okay to kill somebody with a bullet or a bomb but not a missile? Okay to kill him from fifty feet away or fifty miles away but not ten thousand miles away? Seems to me that doesn't make any moral difference to the act of killing – let alone practical one to the guy getting killed.

MEREDITH: Whatever you say. But if this is still supposed to be a democracy shouldn't we be in that room, too?

DOUG: Sure – if politics is just smart talk without practical consequences on that beautiful sloping lawn at Swarthmore – but where real decisions get made about really important issues of life and death in real time –

MEREDITH: We should just let the President jerk off in peace and quiet?

He's stung again –

DOUG: Four hundred strikes and counting. Successes against terror command and control centers in every theatre. Between the White House – us – it – the Pentagon and the military we've – they've – run one of the most effective anti-guerilla warfare efforts of all time.

She's looking out of the window –

MEREDITH: I saw it happen. I was up. Thinking if I really want to keep doing this. The first car was standing there, waiting for the light. The other car was doing sixty, seventy, something like that. Didn't even brake. Hit it head on. A door flies open. Driver's side. Something shoots out. I mean *shoots* out. It's a girl. Hits a lamp post. Bounces off it back into the road. *Bounces.* She tries to get up; reflexes, adrenaline, whatever. Somebody else comes from nowhere – the corner, I guess – and *smack.* Drags her under their car. Twenty, thirty feet. I see everything. I watch it happen. Through the triple glazing there isn't a sound. I'm a hundred feet away but I could be on the moon. Watching. Detached. Calm. Interested. *What's going to happen next?* This thing framed in the window playing out in total silence. *That girl is dead,* I think. *She's toast.* And there's not a sound.

THE LIGHTS SNAP OUT ON THEM and RISE on MAXINE and JAY.

JAY: You really don't have to come in to this meeting today, Maxine. It's as straightforward as they get. Al-Rizvi is an immediate threat; his capture is infeasible while he is on Pakistani territory and the operation conforms with the applicable principles of the laws of war. Done deal. You'll have that little shit from the White House national security team creaming himself thinking about the Rose Garden Press Conference in which the President can announce the elimination of another threat –

MAXINE: He's never a problem but –

JAY: The military? You're worried about them? They may not like the way we've been doing more and more of the heavy lifting with Unmanned Aerial Vehicle warfare but in the case of al-Rizvi –

MAXINE: I'm not worried about getting a Yes from Defense. The problem is –

JAY: The problem is through there –

He indicates the heart monitor –

Your daughter. It's about what she needs, which includes her mom being here when she comes out of the coma.

MAXINE: That could be days away. Or weeks. Or never.

JAY: Don't say that.

MAXINE: Never. Okay? Never. I can't fool myself. That's what I could be looking at. Meantime –

JAY: Meantime Tuesday is just the day we take the garbage out. Last Tuesday, this Tuesday, next Tuesday. This is an easier call than usual and you being there or not won't make any difference to the outcome –

MAXINE: There's a wedding in that village today. We found out a few hours ago. Al-Rizvi is going to be there because it's cover for his meeting with a high ranking Pakistani IS officer.

She sips the coffee, makes a face –

You're right. Lousy coffee.

JAY: If we hit al-Rizvi today we likely kill an ISI agent and the members of a wedding party?

MAXINE: There's more. We have an agent in that village, too. He's our human intel on this one. We can't get him out before the strike so the question is –

JAY: There is no debate here, Maxine. Not as far as Legal is concerned. I can't sanction a strike which is likely to take out – count 'em –

He checks it off on his fingers –

One, an ISI agent.

Two, one of our own assets –

MAXINE: – a Pakistani who is also a British passport holder. In full disclosure –

JAY: – And three, God knows how many members of a wedding party –

MAXINE: – but also a leading figure in an organization which threatens the lives of every single one of us.

JAY: If you push it up a day – let the wedding party break up – give your guy and the ISI guy time to get clear –

MAXINE: We lose track of al-Rizvi. We throw away months of work – years.

JAY: *Wedding Party Blown Up By Drone Attack. Protests At US Embassies Worldwide.* You like those headlines? You like the idea of the British Prime Minister registering a formal protest? That one of their nationals has been taken out without even the courtesy of a phone call to Downing Street.

MAXINE: We could text her.

JAY: Not funny.

MAXINE: It's a tough call for you guys in Legal, I know –

JAY: It's an easy call. No way. Be very clear that Legal will only sanction a strike on al-Rizvi. We will not okay any action which will lead to the death or injury of anyone else. Period.

MAXINE: If we call it a signature strike? On a group of guys associating with a known terrorist?

JAY: Unarmed wedding guests?

MAXINE: Of fighting age? Which gives us adequate reason to suspect their motives for being there?

JAY: Nice try but no dice. You've run out of road, Maxine. You are okayed for a targeted strike on this one man and that's it. But not today.

The lights snap out on them and rise on a middle-aged man, COMMANDER BEN CROWE, in shorts and tee-shirt, playing basketball one-on-one with CAPTAIN MARIO GARCIA –

BEN: Are you really making the case that I go into that meeting and argue against the al-Rizvi strike? Are you nuts? This guy occupies a leadership role in planning co-ordinated attacks like in Paris and Brussels and in encouraging lone wolf attacks globally. He's worked really hard to get on the target list and today's the day we return him to the bosom of his ancestors, courtesy of General Dynamics.

MARIO: Intel puts him five clicks south of the Af-Pac border. There's a chance we could get a Special Forces team in and exfiltrate him. This is the one we could make our stand on. The one we've been looking for. We agreed we have got to get this program back from the spooks. We've stood by for years and seen the drone warfare program virtually taken over by Langley. They should be in the Intelligence business, not dropping bombs on people. We have to get back to where *they* tell the President where the threats are coming from and *we* deal with them.

BEN: To which that really smart woman from the CIA is going to say that the shape of the battlefield changed and Langley understood that faster than the Pentagon did.

MARIO: Those cowboys are going to do what they always do – keep pushing until everything blows up in their faces. The Bay of Pigs? Training death squads in Central America? Helping fake the rationale for the invasion of Iraq?

The clock's ticking. If we're going to nix the strike and authorize the raid –

BEN: Clocks don't tick any more. They hum or something.

You think anybody in that room is going to want to talk about long-term consequences? They want results in the next news cycle.

MARIO: Isn't a major intelligence coup a result?

BEN: You're advocating I should argue for sending other young Americans in Special Forces into harm's way to try to bring this guy in?

MARIO: I am.

BEN: At risk of their lives?

MARIO: Affirmative.

BEN: When we could kill him from thirty-five thousand feet instead?

MARIO: If we do that we lose intelligence that could save many, many more lives.

I've been downrange. I know the jeopardy you'd be putting them in. I've been stood on the x myself. That's what gives me the right to argue this.

BEN: Cool your jets, son. You can't fight this entire war by yourself.

MARIO: I know you may can my ass for this but I ran it by Ops. They're putting together a provisional plan. They know the route al-Rizvi will likely take to get back into Afghanistan. You can argue for a twenty-four hour hold on the kill and send them in to bring him in alive. Hand him over to the CIA and say *We did our job by stalking him and catching him. Now go do yours and find out what he knows.* Leaving your opposite number from Langley standing in a corner adjusting her girdle because somebody has to seriously examine where this program is going before it blows up in all our faces.

BEN: Goddamn –

He throws the ball away –

I don't like this way of fighting a war any more than you do. Maybe what really gets my goat isn't that the CIA are crowding us out but they're doing it in sneakers.

MARIO: Sneakers?

BEN: If you're going to fight a war by computer you might as well do it in Starbucks. Put on a pair of old jeans, order a latte and finish the guy off without a second thought.

I'm not sure my old man would understand this way of fighting a war. When he was wrangling that F16 over Hanoi he was taking an even chance he wouldn't make it back. When he risked his own life he comprehended the stakes for the guy he was setting out to kill.

MARIO: Al-Rizvi –
    Be
    Ever read the Greeks?

MARIO: Sir –?

BEN: Sophocles – Euripides – those guys?

MARIO: No sir.

BEN: Secret vice of mine. Got into it when I had to study Xenophon on a staff course. Sophocles says somewhere that no vast thing comes into the world without a curse.

MARIO: I appreciate that, sir –

BEN sits on a bench and starts to dress in his uniform –

BEN: Sneakers? I hate them. I like an old fashioned full grain leather shoe that will take a nice shine because the care of the shoe is where pride in appearance begins. Especially for those of us who have elected to make our career in the military. It shows respect for that uniform which sets us apart from common humanity because until now it has always been us alone who have been delegated the task of killing without moral judgement; those permitted to break civilization's first rule in order to preserve it.

MARIO: Absolutely, sir but the Al-Rizvi question –?

BEN: I cannot tell my Admiral that I went in that room and called this strike off.

MARIO: Al-Rizvi is the worst of the worst. He's a really difficult case to draw the line on. That's why he's the best case to do that.

BEN: There's a new administration coming in. They may want to review the policy. In the meantime –

MARIO: If we can show the importance of intelligence gathering rather than wholesale assassination –

BEN: Careful –

MARIO: These are extra-judicial killings carried out on the flimsiest of legal pretexts –

BEN's voice is sharp –

BEN: Given the aforesaid new administration it behoves a wise man in such times to look to his own. To consider the fruits of his fields and how high the grain is heaped in his granary.

MARIO: Granary, sir?

BEN: The Admiral is a wise man. He has tended his fields with diligence. His back has been bent in labor over the past few years, to good purpose. He has prospered and made his family rejoice. Now would be a good time to make further provision for himself and them. After thirty years on military pay he has taken counsel of himself and decided that it might be time to move to the private sector. That's where the gravy is.

MARIO: I see –

BEN: You do?

MARIO: Would the Admiral be thinking of a job in the defense industry?

BEN: That's where his expertise is.

MARIO: And his contacts?

BEN: Being a wise man he has taken care to seek the good approval of those around him; hosts sing his praises; he is greeted with shouts of joy in the places where the elect dwell and have their being. His battles have been fought in the halls of Congress and the Pentagon rather than the High Seas and he's spilled more ink than blood. Such a man would not wish the tongues of the evil to whisper against him that he is not to be trusted with great affairs; that he is afraid to loose the arrow of righteousness against the enemies of the Lord –

MARIO: Even if we both agree that al-Rizvi could be one of the greatest intelligence coups ever?

BEN: *(Sharply.)* Don't put words into my mouth.

MARIO: But isn't that right?

BEN: That's the case you're making. Not me.

MARIO: The Admiral is going to be working for one of the corporations that builds these things?

BEN: Powerful men are a cross between spoiled children and homicidal maniacs and should not be questioned too closely.

MARIO: Is he?

BEN: He has a lot to bring to the table for any company attempting to navigate the complexities of the procurement program. A labyrinth even the legendary Theseus would have found daunting. Now I suggest you send for my driver.

MARIO: Has he asked you to go with him? Will you be working for them too?

BEN: Did I ever tell you about the country boy who applied for a job on the railroad?

MARIO: *(Off balance.)* I don't think you did, sir.

BEN: *Imagine you're in charge of the points on a one track line,* it's put to him. *Imagine there's one train travelling South at a hundred miles an hour and another North at a hundred miles an hour and it looks like they're going to collide head on. What would you do?*

The country boy thinks and says *I guess I'd send for my cousin.* He's asked *Why on earth would you do that?* He says *I guess my cousin ain't never seen a train wreck before.*

Another steely look at MARIO –

BEN: You ask me that question again, son and your career's about to be a train wreck –

THE LIGHTS FADE ON THEM and rise on MAXINE and JAY –

MAXINE: How's Jane?

JAY: Jane?

MAXINE: I saw her at the clinic in Bethesda when I was picking up Brittany after her last re-hab.

JAY: *(Wary.)* She drops by there from time to time. She made a lot of friends on the staff. It's a social thing. She doesn't have that problem any more.

MAXINE: They have an oxycontin addiction clinic. If she's going there –

JAY: She's not.

MAXINE: – if she's going there and you kept it off your security questionnaire you could lose your clearances. I would hate that to happen to you, Jay. That would be a career changer. No more government service. No more being where the power is.

JAY: She had a little slip-up.

MAXINE: Which you reported. No doubt. So it's not a problem, is it?

He hesitates –

JAY: You want this that bad?

MAXINE: I always thought you were an ally in that room.

JAY: You just told me –

MAXINE: I didn't tell you anything. Not yet. We just grabbed a coffee. If I go into a meeting and my head's still back here with my desperately sick daughter –

She indicates the ward –

MAXINE: – and in all that's going on with her I forget to flag the file about the wedding party and the asset, that's on me.

JAY: They'll still fire you. It would come out sooner or later.

MAXINE: I'm tired anyway, Jay. I am so, so tired – of being a single mom – the workload – a war that keeps changing shape, without definition of what winning or losing might be – having to keep coming up with reasons to sign off on targets and strikes and never be totally sure, not fifty percent sometimes; never a hundred; rarely even eighty

21

percent *sure* – but I'm sure about this one. Whatever the risks.

JAY: Just as long as we're clear they're all going to die because you feel guilty about the times you couldn't be a mom to your kid.

MAXINE: Say that again.

JAY: Isn't that true?

MAXINE: Al-Rizvi is going to die because he's a son of a bitch. My focus is on him and that's where yours should be –

Before he can respond there's a urgent beeping sound and they turn to see the heart rate monitor go flat and then show only a faint, troubled, irregular beat as the LIGHTS FADE ON THEM and RISE on DOUG and MEREDITH. They're dressed for the street and he's trying to hail a cab –

DOUG: Fucking uber driver. Taxi!

He watches it go past –

Maybe I should walk. Be fifteen, twenty minutes, tops.

MEREDITH: Do you phone her on the way in? From the taxi? Usually? *Hi honey. How did you sleep? How are the kids?* Or do you wait until after? Tell her she's not to worry, you slept like a log and you were the smartest guy in a room of very smart guys. Any women in there?

DOUG: One.

Shit.

I didn't say that.

MEREDITH: Is that a strange job for a woman? Deciding who gets bug-zapped? *Zzzzp. Zzzzp. Zzzzp.*

DOUG: What these people stand for is as much a war on women as it is on anything.

MEREDITH: I'd like to meet her.

DOUG: For some people in DC poli-science isn't a four year indulgence. It's what they spend their lives doing. In jobs where there are real consequences.

MEREDITH: She's your killer chick?

DOUG: I'm going to walk.

MEREDITH: She's Bonnie and you're Clyde? Or do you take it in turns to go on top?

DOUG: Is it possible for you ever to reach for a metaphor that isn't sexual?

MEREDITH: Isn't a Hellfire missile the biggest and angriest dick you ever saw?

DOUG: Should I walk?

MEREDITH: You're going to make a choice between life and death in a few minutes and you can't even work out the pluses and minuses of foot versus taxi?

Indicates his sneakers –

Nice sneakers, by the way. Did Holly choose them? Does she know about us? Has she guessed there's somebody else?

DOUG: I don't think so.

MEREDITH: You can't be sure of what your own wife is thinking a few minutes away from here but you have every confidence you're aware of what's happening on the other side of the world; where somebody gets to live, somebody gets to die depending on the call you make?

He sees a taxi –

There's a –

He waves his hand but the taxi fails to stop –

Hey! –

Indignant, he turns to follow its progress and sees the wreckage of the accident –

Wow. You were right about that car crash last night. I slept through that?

MEREDITH: I told you. No sound. It was like watching one of those video clips where you see the cockpit footage of your guys blowing something up. Just the puff of smoke.

DOUG: That's raw footage. There's no context. Just like this –

He gestures at the scene –

DOUG: Car. Lamp post. Sidewalk.

MEREDITH: Street. Puff of smoke. Dead bodies.

DOUG: Those are nouns, Meredith. They don't add up to a sentence. There's no narrative to hold them in place and explain what happened. You need the why. The who. The what. *The context.*

MEREDITH: So give me the context.

DOUG: Watch CNN tonight. Okay?

MEREDITH: You get reviewed? *Four stars out of five. Two thumbs up. A real crowd pleaser. Doug Gibson in the role of idealistic young White House policy wonk turned apologist for the drone program gave a particularly effective performance.*

DOUG: To understand it you need names. Back story. You have to explain why the first car was there. Why the other car didn't brake. Why the third car didn't stop in time. Who the girl who was thrown out was. We don't know any of that. It's just broken glass.

MEREDITH: Or dead bodies in Pakistan or the Yemen or Iraq.

DOUG: Some of the smartest people in the world are paid to tell us who and why and when and where.

MEREDITH: They're never wrong?

DOUG: Sometimes.

MEREDITH: And –?

DOUG: This time? No.

MEREDITH: If they were –?

DOUG: I know why I'm in DC. I know why I'm in government service and I accept the box I have to live my life in, okay?

She raises her arm –

MEREDITH: *Et voila.* I got you a taxi.

DOUG: Next Monday? And I can maybe grab a couple of days later in the week. Holly's taking the kids to her parents.

MEREDITH: Is that what you were talking to her about last night? You phoned her when I was in the shower. The shower was running. You took that chance. The chance she'd hear it. The chance I'd walk back into the room and say something and she'd ask *who's that?*

DOUG: I was tired, not thinking straight –

MEREDITH: You took that risk. Then you hurt your hand when you punched the wall when we argued about it. Just for a moment there, you were out of control Doug.

DOUG: I apologized for that and I was not out of control –

MEREDITH: Tonight you're going to take the metro home – not forgetting to pick up the milk – walk nine blocks, take a look at the fucking roses you love so much, head inside the house, drop your briefcase, hug your wife, grab your kids, share a meal, put them to bed, watch some TV, shower, put the lights out and go to sleep knowing you killed a man today.

DOUG: Next Monday?

MEREDITH: You don't even have the excuse that you're a nineteen-year-old farm boy in uniform, who's fried his brains on *Mortal Kombat*.

DOUG: The driver's waiting –

MEREDITH: How is this not driving you crazy? By what – evasion – by what – mental trick – by what – defenestration of your intellect – ethnic cleansing of your conscience – machine-gunning of all human decency – can you, of all people, do that and live with it –?

The lights snap out on them, rising on JAY and MAXINE –

JAY: I drove in past the Capitol last night. They're getting it ready for the Inauguration. We might get away with the next one but the one after might have to be held underground behind ten feet of concrete and steel because this thing is out of our control now and maybe the President won't even be safe there because these things are getting smaller and smaller and one day you'll be able to send one through a keyhole or under the door packed with enough explosive to bring a building down.

You think we can contain this thing now? Seriously? We haven't only pioneered the technology of how the wars of the future will be fought – fuck us very much for that – we are in the process of legitimizing a form of warfare that means nobody is going to be safe, not in any street, not in any building, not in any room, not anywhere – we are going to be at the mercy of every chickenshit Third World dictatorship or theocracy obsessed with apocalypse and even one freelance lunatic with a grudge can exit his mother's basement to bring the same kind of wholesale terror to us as you're planning today.

MAXINE: Not terror –

He loses it –

JAY: *Christ on a fucking stick, Maxine what the hell else _is_ it?*

The lights rise on BEN and MARIO –

BEN: *I have learned to obey the commands*
Of our gods and to respect the authority
Of the House of Atreus. They are our leaders,
And we, mere subordinates, should submit.
What other way is there? Neither the dread
Nor the mighty powers are exempt
From this rule. Thus Winter with her snowy feet
Defers to the warmth of Summer's roots, and Night,
Tired from his lonely trek, withdraws
Before the white steeds of Day. Ajax. One of the greatest
Greek warriors but Sophocles' Ajax is a vain and jealous
man who at one point realizes that he has been responsible
for the deaths of innocent people. Bystanders. Civilians.
Non-combatants.

MARIO: Which is one of the inevitable dangers of this strike.
Which is why you have to make a stand against it –

BEN: *As you were.*

He's said it with something like the savagery of command, then steadies himself –

BEN: He is however a man of honor and overcome with
shame at what he's done, feeling that he has forfeited
that honor by those deaths, Ajax takes the sword of a
vanquished hero, Hector and plants it in the ground facing
upwards –

Ye springs and streams, and Trojan plains,
Farewell, all ye who have sustained my life.
This is the last word Ajax speaks to you.
All else in Hades to the dead will I say.

He falls on the sword.

A beat –

BEN: File –

He holds out his hand and takes a file from BEN, hesitates –

BEN: Then again it's a very old play and I'm not sure that I'm about to fall on my sword, yet, son.

The lights rise on MAXINE and JAY –

MAXINE: Got it. Your objections noted and filed. A policy issue. Not operations. None of my business. Now I need an answer. When we go in today will you be outside the tent pissing in or inside the tent pissing out –?

Before he can answer the heart monitor gives a steady beep and the display flat-lines. She closes her eyes, steadies herself, opens them –

MAXINE: I have a decision to make…

As she braces herself to make that life-or-death decision about her daughter, the LIGHTS hold on BEN and DOUG on their way to make another life-or-death decision and we GO TO BLACKOUT and –

– end –

FROM A VERBATIM INTERVIEW WITH CLIVE STAFFORD
SMITH O.B.E. DIRECTOR OF REPRIEVE.

EDITED BY NICOLAS KENT
SEPTEMBER 2016

I am Clive Stafford Smith, the director of Reprieve, and I've been talking about Drones for days – *(with a laugh in his voice)* I'm claiming that I coined the phrase the Drone Age, like the Stone Age.

We know [that there are regular Tuesday targeting meetings at the White House] as a matter of fact; as they said it *and* they boasted about it. They said how it happened, the President of the United States sits there, and they have a power point display where he is shown the pictures of who they might want to kill this week and he, much like Nero, he does a yea or nay with his thumb.

It is certainly true that the CIA has its own Drone programme, [the Pentagon and the CIA] both operate on the border between Afghanistan and Waziristan. According to what they've released, the military which is supposedly more open, not very open but slightly more open, has a code of conduct that is fairly specific. The CIA has no such oversight whatsoever, has no code of conduct, and President Obama waived the rules for the CIA so if you are doing something that is totally illegal, as opposed to just pretty illegal, then the rules are much looser, and you can do worse things.

In terms of criminal law [the U.S.] has a line of defence: they are the ones who prosecute themselves; so as long as they have established the rules that they can't be prosecuted – they are okay. So the U.S. has not signed on [to] the International Criminal Court so we cannot prosecute them there, and the [U.S.] Attorney General who has signed off on this whole process in the first place, that all this is legal, is not going to prosecute people in America for what they did – so there is simply no way that these people are likely to get prosecuted there.

The Drones programme is utterly counter-productive; so for an example according to recent figures we have, for every HVT – high value target – they target they never get them first time. There is one chap, Baitullah Mesud, they have targeted seventeen times – you know a cat has nine lives, this guy has seventeen. On average they kill nine innocent children for each person they target – now I have got an eight year old – so you can imagine what that does to these communities, to kill all these children. There was this intelligence officer who said, in 2004, that for every Guantanamo prisoner we have provoked ten people to want to kill us. It is way more than that in the context of Drones, for every one individual we have killed we have provoked a whole community.

We studied one particular group of people. For the whole figure of those they were targeting, it was 1437 people they had killed in an effort to target forty-seven people, and among those there were scores and scores of kids – that was in 2014 – that study was primarily in Wazaristan.

[In terms of compensation] if you are in Afghanistan, a real war zone, then there is a methodology, then they have a way that they calculate it. My favourite statistic from that is that if you are a cow in Afghanistan and you get killed you get $300– if you are a human being in Pakistan you get nothing.

What we are talking about is the unrecognised problems about how Drones reduce the threshold at which we are willing to go to war.

So it is one thing to send troops in where an American or British person might come home in a body bag, I don't want that, but that makes you pause before you do it, it is another thing to send in an F16, [a pilot] might get captured, then it is a huge international incident, but when you are talking only about a drone you can sit in Creech air force base in Nevada, and play your video games with your cup of coffee and do things on the other side of the world with absolutely zero possibility that any Americans are going to get hurt. I don't want Americans to get hurt, but at the same time that means that people say "Drones baby Drones" when they are asked about [the future of] warfare.

The British do have a kill list – they have announced they have a kill list. Theirs is bizarrely very very different in concept to the Americans. The British kill list is almost uniquely focused on British nationals which is odd – the Americans are very leery about killing Americans, because they have constitutional rights – the British are only killing British people. The British are focused exclusively on propagandists [like Mohammed Emwazi – Jihadi John]. If you look at the British list it is focused entirely on your column inches in a tabloid newspaper, and it is relatively small and they follow a process where they sanction you at the UN first. What the British have done with the next four targets they have – is they have listed them in the UN sanctioned target list and you know these are the people that they are now targeting to kill.

GCHQ in Cheltenham is intimately involved all around the world with the Americans. So *we are not* pushing the button of the hellfire missile every time but *we are* part of the Mafia of killing people in all sorts of places – the Brits are up to their necks in all of this.

[Square brackets denote additions inserted for clarity]

THE KID

Characters

SHAWNA
PETE
RAMON
ALICE

The living room of PETE and ALICE's American suburban home.

Shawna
Pete
Ramon
Alice

Two couples, each in their thirties.

PETE: We shouldn't really talk about it.

RAMON: Come on, Pete, it's been on CNN. We know it was you guys.

PETE: Well…

SHAWNA: Pete.

PETE: What can we say?

SHAWNA: We're not supposed to say anything.

RAMON: Come on guys!

PETE: Well… I think we can say… can we say this?

SHAWNA doesn't respond.

PETE: A certain event which you may, or may not have heard about in the news…

RAMON: …yes…

PETE: … in which a senior Taliban commander was killed…

RAMON: …yes…

PETE: …may or may not have been a Reaper drone mission flown from here in Creech, which may or may not be the base from which Shawna and I operate.

RAMON: …yes…and…

PETE: …well let's put it this way, that successful mission, may or may not, have been flown on the shift we just worked.

RAMON: Bam!

RAMON laughs.

SHAWNA: It really is no big deal.

RAMON: It's a very big deal.

ALICE: I think it's a big deal.

PETER: Honestly.

RAMON: Come on!

PETER: We were just doing our job.

RAMON: I love it! 'Doing our job.'

PETER: Well –

RAMON: You took out one of the top bad guys in the world.

PETER: I know but –

RAMON: I think that deserves a moment of congratulation.

SHAWNA: A moment of reflection maybe.

RAMON: A moment of celebration.

SHAWNA: Celebration?

RAMON: Yes. Celebration. Of course celebration.

ALICE: I agree.

RAMON: See.

A toast!

To Pete and Shawna.

RAMON & ALICE: Pete and Shawna!

ALICE: American heroes.

RAMON: American heroes.

SHAWNA: It's embarrassing.

RAMON: Bullshit, baby. It's not embarrassing. I'll tell you what's embarrassing. What's embarrassing is how little praise you guys get. How little recognition. You get up at crazy hours of the day or night to work shifts. You stay focused for eight hours straight. You patrol the skies all over the world. You protect us. But do we hear about you guys on the news? Do you guys get purple hearts? No?

That's what's embarrassing.

PETE: How about this.

To a successful mission.

RAMON: …

Okay.

Cool.

To a successful mission.

ALL: To a successful mission.

All raise glasses and chink.

A moment.

PETE: You know who the real heroes are?

RAMON: No.

PETE: You.

You guys.

We are so lucky, Shawna and me, to have such supportive partners.

We appreciate it.

We really do.

PETE kisses ALICE.

RAMON kisses SHAWNA.

ALICE: We're so glad you two could come tonight.

PETE: It means a lot to us, really.

ALICE: You're our oldest friends.

RAMON: Old. Speak for yourself! I'm twenty-two!

Laughter.

PETE: Seriously.

>This is one of those days you see everything in perspective.

>Look at us!

>Good jobs. In a good suburb. Good friends. Good partners.

RAMON: Good food!

ALICE: Great country.

RAMON: Warm night.

PETE: Warm friendship.

SHAWNA: Warm white wine.

RAMON: Don't bitch, baby.

SHAWNA: It was a joke.

RAMON: They don't know that.

PETE: You forget, Ramon, I know her too well.

>She's my pilot.

RAMON: Seriously.

PETE: Seriously. Let's raise a glass.

SHAWNA: Can we just drink.

PETER: To Life!

ALL: To Life!

SHAWNA: To life…

We're probably going to need another bottle.

A moment.

RAMON: Okay, so, tell me about assassinating a senior Taliban commander.

SHAWNA: We're not allowed to talk about it.

RAMON: I know you're not allowed to talk about it but –

PETE: We're not allowed to talk about it specifically but we can talk about it generally.

RAMON: Okay, generally, assassinating a senior Taliban commander…

PETE: Yeah…?

RAMON: What's it like?

A moment.

SHAWNA: Go ahead.

PETE: Well, the first thing to say is that this is not a video game. The level of control, the variables – wind, visibility, sandstorms – you know – this is complex stuff, and, this may sound weird, but when we're flying it really feels like we're flying. We feel the plane's movement in our bodies.

You know.

It's real.

Mostly we're on patrol. We circle high up over an area, use the camera to track vehicles, make observations. We read the intel scroll at the side of the screen: feeds coming in from the grunts on the ground, from other agency offices, from the military. As I say. Mostly it's surveillance. But sometimes we're given a target.

That's different.

We take the briefing information. We fly to the target area and try to get an ident. Once we've got one confirmed, we wait for a chance at a clear shot. When that moment comes we put out a call for permissions – refer to legal – presuming everyone's happy. Shawna pilots the approach, I lock targets with the hellfires and we're go.

It's a lot of procedure but the logic is pretty straight forward.

This time – the target's at a wedding. We watch, we wait, we watch. A lotta coffee. The party goes on into the night. Finally, at dawn, we see him. He comes out of a hut. This is just near the end of our shift. He comes out of a hut, he scratches his ass, he stands and he looks at the view. Sun's rising over the mountains.

You have to admit it's beautiful.

He's drinking from a little coffee cup and under his arm there's a newspaper. These guys don't use phones or kindles or anything. Those things leave traces – so these guys are just about the last guys in the world who still use the print media for information.

Anyway, there he is, plain as you like, like grandpa Walton. Only this is a guy who has – and I don't know the details – but this guy has been responsible for the deaths of hundreds of innocent people.

Shawna spotted it. Couple of days ago she says to me: 'Yesterday morning, did you notice, yesterday morning at half past eight he picked up a newspaper and walked to the outhouse. Did you notice?' I say hadn't but now she mentions it…. Then she says 'You realise what he was doing?'

And that's when we realise.

Oh my god.

He's going for a dump.

RAMON: Oh my god.

Fuck. Fantastic.

PETE: Exactly.

ALICE: Why is it fantastic?

PETE: It's good because we know the outhouse is way over in a corner of the compound. It's morning. Everyone's still in bed. Now we know we have a window of one, two maybe five minutes when he's going to be in there, pants round his ankles, ass over a hole, alone.

Boom.

RAMON: Poor guy.

PETE: Exactly.

So we alert Intel. Intel sends it to legal.

Clear blue sky.

The instruction comes up on the feed – 'Go'.

Shawna wheels us round for an approach, I lock, fix and –

There's this thing I always do when I press the button.

'I am the god of hellfire and I bring you –

Fire!

PETE mimes pressing the button.

PETE makes the noise of a missile.

PETE makes the noise of an explosion.

RAMON: Woah.

Amazing, truly amazing.

SHAWNA: It's just a system.

ALICE: A system which works.

PETE: Exactly.

Which is why we're winning. You see, we don't fight wars anymore. We process information. No blundering into compounds with special forces. No need for terrified women and children. No need for injuries, rapes, videos of beheaded G.Is. No need for any of that shit.

Just one clean shot and

Mission accomplished.

RAMON: *(Raises glass.)* Mission accomplished.

A moment.

ALICE: I'm proud of you. Proud of you both.

RAMON: Me too.

ALICE: Proud of America.

RAMON: Proud of democracy.

PETE: Jeez!

RAMON: Yes – proud of democracy – yes –

SHAWNA: Ramon –

RAMON: Let me speak baby

SHAWNA: Okay but –

RAMON: I'm serious. It's because of democracy that we invented these weapons. And the purpose of these weapons is to kill LESS people, not more. When you think about that, when you think about the distance you people go to, to make sure you get these kills right: the agency, the air force, the president all working to make sure only the bad guys get whacked.

When I think of that I feel proud of democracy.

SHAWNA: Ramon –

RAMON: Maybe it's the wine but I feel emotional about that.

SHAWNA: We don't only get the bad.

RAMON: Okay but we mostly get the bad.

SHAWNA: Sometimes.

RAMON: Mostly.

PETER: I don't know if we only get the bad but I think it's fair to say we kill less of the not bad than any other currently available weapons system.

SHAWNA: We make mistakes –

PETE: One civilian death for every 120 terrorist, that's pretty discriminating.

SHAWNA: Depending on your definition of terrorist.

ALICE: What does that mean?

SHAWNA: It means if your definition of terrorist is somebody who happens to be killed by a drone then...

PETE: Shawna, that's not fair –

SHAWNA: Isn't it?

RAMON: But look at what's possible now. I mean, you guys can see a Taliban, you can see he's sitting in the shade, you can even read the fucking headline of his newspaper for Christ sake –

PETE: We can't read the headline.

RAMON: You can see him

PETE: We didn't know that, we interpreted that.

RAMON: You might as well be able to see inside the bastard's head.

PETER: One day maybe that is something we'll be able to do.

SHAWNA: We already read their fucking facebook updates.

RAMON: Exactly – so then the poor guy goes to sit on the john and – boom.

PETE: Boom.

ALICE: Boom.

RAMON: It's amazing.

PETE: It's satisfying – I admit that.

RAMON: Boom.

A moment.

SHAWNA: There is no boom.

RAMON: Okay.

SHAWNA: The screen pixellates.

RAMON: Okay.

SHAWNA: That's how we know the missile's hit.

The image dissolves.

There isn't sound.

PETE: The sound is ten thousand miles away.

RAMON: Of course.

A moment.

ALICE: But they hear sound?

PETE: Who?

ALICE: Them.

PETE: Oh, yeah, of course.

Maybe not the guy getting wasted but –

The near bystanders.

They would certainly hear a bang.

ALICE: Is it a loud bang?

PETE: Very.

SHAWNA: Fucking very.

PETE: A fucking very, very, very loud bang.

RAMON laughs.

SHAWNA: We need another bottle.

She goes to get another bottle.

A moment.

She comes back.

RAMON: Do you ever see funny stuff?

PETE: Funny stuff?

RAMON: You know, like bloopers.

PETE: Not really, I don't think.

SHAWNA: Sometimes.

RAMON: Sometimes?

SHAWNA: Sometimes we see funny stuff.

RAMON: Like what?

PETE: Just life. Just people doing their thing.

SHAWNA: Once we saw a couple fucking.

RAMON: Wow! For real?

ALICE: You didn't tell me this.

PETE: Didn't I?

ALICE: No!

PETE: Shawna.

SHAWNA: Fuck it. Why not? It happened, didn't it?

We were on a mission, over a village, nothing much happening, cockerel pecking about in the yard, women beating laundry, men playing backgammon. It's hot, you know. Everyone's staying still. So the slightest movement – it draws the eye. Which is when Pete says, 'what's that?' I say – 'Where?'. 'There' he says, and he hones in on the roof. It takes a minute but then I see it. A little pair of Tali-buttocks swinging back and forth and, in front of them, a boy on his knees. Some kinky mullah was showing this kid the true meaning of jihad.

RAMON: Tali buttocks!

SHAWNA: I thought that was funny.

ALICE: What did you do?

SHAWNA: We watched!

PETE: The comments were choice.

ALICE: Comments?

PETE: From the intel guys, the grunts watching the feed.

ALICE: You shared this?

SHAWNA: There's not a lot to do in the skies above Waziristan.

ALICE: Couldn't you have looked away?

SHAWNA: It passed the time.

ALICE: It's a little distasteful, isn't it?

SHAWNA: Distasteful?

ALICE: If I was that boy.

SHAWNA: You're not.

ALICE: But I could be – one could be.

SHAWNA: But you're not.

ALICE: I know but… the ideas that someone was watching that from above.

RAMON: What about god?

ALICE: God?

RAMON: Mullah must have thought god was watching him from above.

That didn't bother him.

So what's the problem?

ALICE: I just think it's distasteful.

A moment.

SHAWNA: He was probably being raped.

ALICE: What?

SHAWNA: The fucker was a guy we were following.

Preacher.

The boy was some kid.

We watched because I half thought we might get a chance at a clear shot.

A moment.

ALICE: Sorry.

SHAWN: No, I'm sorry.

It was.

It was an inappropriate story.

Distasteful, you're right.

A moment.

PETE: The trouble is, 40000 feet up and hellfire is too crude for that kind of policing.

In future it'll be easier.

The way the technology is going, drones are getting smaller and smaller. There are drones now as small as buzzards. Pretty soon we're going to have drones size of song birds. The next level – if they can work out the optics – is drones the size of bees.

Then you can police rape.

We could establish the intel, fly in over the compound wall, past the laundry women, up the stairs, over the roof, right up in front of his face – confirm it's the right guy then – zap – in at the eye socket and we blow his skull right open.

ALICE: What would happen to the boy.

PETE: Splash of blood.

He'd hardly notice except for the fact the old man just keeled over.

A moment.

RAMON: I don't know.

It's a nice picture but –

We still need boots on the ground.

The grunts.

Don't we?

PETE: Do we?

RAMON: In the end. You need muscle. Don't you?

Some guy with muscles patrolling the street.

PETE: Drones can patrol the street.

The more we can do with drones the better. Drone guards. Drone soldiers. Drone planes. Drone ships. Drone submarines.

The whole shebang.

We could have an army of drones out there, and back here hundreds of us in shorts, on coloured bean bags, operating joysticks – like Google campus.

What you doing? – Sorry Brian I can't talk – I'm in hand to hand combat with an insurgent right now – I just need to cut his throat – excuse me – ewww. – I'm done. High five. Time for a chai latte?

SHAWNA: Not chai latte.

PETE: What?

SHAWNA: It wouldn't be a chai latte.

It would be Espresso.

Caffeine.

Drone operators love caffeine.

ALICE: You make it sound fun.

PETE: It could be fun.

RAMON: Canteen,

Massage therapy,

Ping pong.

If that was the army you wouldn't need conscription.

PETE: That's the beauty of it. You wouldn't need soldiers at all.

A moment.

ALICE: What about the enemy?

PETE: What about them?

ALICE: What if they get drones?

PETE: Then it's drones v drones.

RAMON: Spy v. Spy.

PETE: We'll be here.

RAMON: They'll be there.

ALICE: So where will the war be.

PETE: I don't know, some desert somewhere.

A moment.

RAMON: The only thing is…

> Couldn't someone come onto your CIA campus which
> I'm guessing is now a google style hangout with ping pong
> tables and espresso machines and just – you know – with
> a knife – or a gun – just – gadda gadda gadda – beanbags
> everywhere – everyone dead.

PETE: I guess.

RAMON: So you would need security.

PETE: Yes.

RAMON: Guards.

PETE: Of course.

RAMON: Guards to guard the drone operators?

> In other words – the army.

PETE: Okay. I get it.

RAMON: War always comes down to muscle in the end.

PETE: I take your point.

RAMON: Guys like me.

PETE: Guys like you.

RAMON: Muscle.

PETE: Muscle.

RAMON laughs.

RAMON and PETE shake hands.

PETE: A toast.

> To the US Army!

ALL: To the US Army!

A moment.

RAMON: So, anyway,

> Enough office talk.

> You guys said you had news.

PETE: We do have news.

> That's why we invited you here.

> Wait!

> For this we need Champagne!

PETE goes off to get Champagne.

A moment.

He comes back.

> Champagne.

> Vintage.

RAMON: Classy.

PETE pops the cork.

PETE pours.

ALICE: Not for me.

RAMON: So, come on, guys, what is it?

> New house?

> You two finally getting hitched?

> What's the big secret?

PETE: Alice…?

ALICE: Let's put it this way. A certain person round this table may – or may not be pregnant. And that person may or may not be me.

A moment.

ALICE squeals.

ALICE: I'm pregnant!!

Yaay!!

PETE: We're going to have a baby.

RAMON: Oh my god! That's wonderful. Congratulations!

SHAWNA: Congratulations.

Hugs.

ALICE: Thank you.

RAMON: Well done you guys!

SHAWNA: Yeah, well done.

RAMON: It's amazing.

PETE: Well – not that amazing.

RAMON: I know but – !

PETE: A little sperm drone.

Swimming along.

It wasn't exactly work.

ALICE: Not work? Are you kidding? Did you see the yoga positions I had to do? The science? The reading. Getting pregnant's a full-time job these days, am I right, Shawna?

SHAWNA: What?

ALICE: Am I right?

SHAWNA: Oh.

Yeah. I guess.

I wouldn't know.

ALICE: Trust me.

A moment.

RAMON: Shawna's upset because we've never had what she calls 'time' for a baby.

SHAWNA: I'm not upset.

RAMON: Clearly, you are upset.

SHAWNA: I'm not upset. Honestly. I'm truly –

I'm happy for you. A kid is a joyful thing. I can't wait to meet it – him – her.

ALICE: It's a him.

We peeked.

She shows the picture of the scan.

All look.

SHAWNA: He's beautiful.

Beautiful.

RAMON: A toast!

To the kid.

ALL: To the kid.

They clink glasses.

SHAWNA: To the kid!

SHAWNA accidentally knocks her glass off the table, it smashes.

SHAWNA: Shit!

Glass on the floor.

RAMON: Careful!

SHAWNA: I'm so sorry!

ALICE: I've got it.

ALICE goes to pick up the glass.

PETE: Leave it.

ALICE: Ow.

PETE: What?

ALICE: I cut myself.

SHAWNA: Oh shit, I'm so sorry.

ALICE: It's fine. It's tiny.

RAMON: You're bleeding.

ALICE: It just a nick.

RAMON: Are you sure there isn't any glass in there.

He examines.

ALICE: I'm sure.

RAMON: Maybe you need antiseptic.

ALICE: I'll wrap it in a napkin.

PETE: Baby. You don't need a napkin, you need hot water and a band aid.

Come on –

First aid kit's in the bathroom. Let's fix you up.

SHAWNA: I'm so sorry.

ALICE: It's okay.

It's quite okay.

PETE: Excuse us.

PETE and ALICE leave.

A moment.

RAMON: What's up with you?

SHAWNA: What do you mean what's up with me?

RAMON: Why are you being so rude?

SHAWNA: I'm not being rude.

RAMON: You are being rude.

SHAWNA: How am I being rude?

RAMON: You're being silent.

SHAWNA: I'm not being silent?

    I'm speaking.

RAMON: You're being withdrawn.

SHAWNA: I'm not withdrawn.

RAMON: Well you have to admit, you're not exactly in the party spirit.

SHAWNA: What should I be doing?

RAMON: You should be cooing.

SHAWNA: Cooing?

RAMON: Cooing.

SHAWNA: I'm not a fucking pigeon.

RAMON: Alice is having a baby.

SHAWNA: I don't know how to coo.

RAMON: Yes you do.

SHAWNA: How do you coo then? You tell me.

RAMON: Ask her if she's bought bootees. Ask her if she's decorated the fucking nursery.

SHAWNA: You ask her.

RAMON: I'm the man.

I'm the fucking man, Shawna.

This is basic stuff.

You coo and I buy Pete a cigar and ask him what kind of car he's thinking of driving.

SHAWNA: He's thinking of driving a Volvo.

RAMON: What?

SHAWNA: He's thinking of driving a Volvo.

RAMON: A Volvo?

SHAWNA: Mileage. Safety. Space in the trunk.

RAMON: A Swedish car.

SHAWNA: Apparently so.

RAMON: Did he tell you this?

SHAWNA: He told me.

RAMON: You talk about what kind of car he's thinking of driving?

SHAWNA: There's not a lot else to talk about when you're flying over Waziristan eight hours a day.

We cover things.

A moment.

RAMON: Do you cover us?

SHAWNA: Us?

RAMON: Do you talk about us?

SHAWNA: Why would we talk about us?

RAMON: Why were you talking about his car?

SHAWNA: I don't know.

    We were looking at the jeeps the Taliban were driving.

    He brought it up.

    It's not a big thing.

RAMON: Have you fucked him?

SHAWNA: Don't be a dick Ramon.

RAMON: Is that what this is about?

SHAWNA: This?

RAMON: This.

    The way you've been lately.

SHAWNA: How have I been lately.

RAMON: Uptight.

SHAWNA: That's not why I'm uptight.

RAMON: Why are you uptight?

    Is it because we're not fucking?

SHAWNA: I'm not uptight. I'm just – tired.

RAMON: Tired waggling a joystick all day?

SHAWNA: It's not a fucking video game!

RAMON: I know. I know.

    You tell me.

    I know.

SHAWNA: I am not fucking Pete.

RAMON: I bet you think about it though.

SHAWNA: I think about a lot of stuff, Ramon.

RAMON: What are you thinking about right now.

SHAWNA: I'm thinking about getting drunk.

She pours wine.

PETE and ALICE return.

PETE: All fixed up.

ALICE: No harm done.

SHAWNA: Is it alright?

ALICE: It's fine.

RAMON: You need some help?

PETE: No, I'm okay, thanks.

SHAWNA: So Alice.

Have you decorated the nursery yet.

ALICE: Well, it's funny you should say that because I was going to ask your advice. I was thinking about colours and I thought – we should go bright, you know? – stripes or circles but then I thought – how long are we necessarily going to be here?

SHAWNA: How long will we be here?

ALICE: Yes.

SHAWNA: How long are we going to be alive?

ALICE: How long are we going to be in this neighborhood.

In this house.

Will we even be here in six months' time?

I mean this house is a lieutenant's house.

But Pete and you, you're such a great team.

I was wondering if …

Pete's always so modest.

But I wondered if maybe as well as expecting a baby

We should be expecting –

She mouths.

Promotion.

PETE: Alice.

ALICE: Well?

After today.

After the news.

I thought maybe we might see a little… thankyou.

From high up.

PETE: A bonus would be nice.

RAMON: Do they do that?

PETE: They sometimes do that.

RAMON: We could do with some spare cash, for sure.

PETE: If a mission is particularly successful.

RAMON: It's only fair.

PETE: I suppose this mission was quite particular.

RAMON: It was on the news.

ALICE: So…

A moment.

SHAWNA: We won't get a bonus.

PETE: We might.

SHAWNA: We won't.

PETE: Why not?

SHAWNA: There was a mistake.

PETE: We hit the target.

SHAWNA: We hit the target but there was a mistake.

PETE: What kind of mistake.

SHAWNA: Collateral.

PETE: Collateral?

ALICE: What's collateral?

SHAWNA: We killed a kid.

A moment.

PETE: What?

SHAWNA: We killed a kid.

I saw him on final approach – he was playing with a stick and a wheel in the corner of the compound – he hadn't been there before – he must have come out of one of the huts – he was chasing the wheel – he was moving towards the lavatory hut.

I was about to say something –

He was running.

And then you fired.

We fired.

A moment.

RAMON: They didn't say this on the news.

PETE: You didn't mention – not even – I mean – a word…

SHAWNA: What was the point.

PETE: To tell me.

SHAWNA: I put it in the written report.

The kid's dead.

I didn't see any point in you losing sleep over it.

PETE: But you're telling me now.

SHAWNA: Only because you were going on about promotion.

RAMON: Why didn't they say this on the news?

SHAWNA: Why do you think Ramon?

Why do you fucking think?

They don't want people to know we kill kids.

That's why.

PETE: Fuck.

SHAWNA: It's not important.

PETE: It is important.

SHAWNA: It's nothing.

PETE: It's not nothing.

SHAWNA: In the scheme of things it's nothing.

PETE: The scheme of things?

SHAWNA: It's collateral.

PETE: It's a kid.

SHAWNA: It was a kid.

Now it's collateral.

A moment.

SHAWNA: I'm sorry.

PETE: I think I'm going to throw up.

Excuse me.

He leaves.

SHAWNA: Wait.

SHAWNA leaves.

A moment.

RAMON: I'm sorry.

ALICE: It's okay.

RAMON: She's tired.

ALICE: I know.

RAMON: She doesn't sleep. She tries to sleep in the day but she can't. I made special coverings for the windows so the bedroom is totally dark. I put insulation in the ceiling to muffle sound. I put the bulb onto a timer so it's like a slow fade, like sundown. We downloaded some of that meditational music. She goes to bed. She tries to sleep. But every time, just as she's falling asleep, she dreams she's dropping out of the sky – and she wakes up. Thump. Time after time. She sleeps eventually, but it's exhausted sleep you know. Not refreshing sleep. I tell her she should think about applying for a transfer, so she can work days. But she says this is what she's good at. She's good at being a pilot. And she likes Pete. So. But – you know – every time – thump – scream – thump – scream. It's not easy.

ALICE: Have you tried Ambien?

RAMON: Ambien?

ALICE: That's what Pete uses.

400 milligrams Ambien.

It works.

RAMON: I'll try it.

PETE and SHAWNA return.

ALICE: You okay?

PETE: I'm okay.

ALICE: Want some water?

PETE: No, it's okay.

ALICE: It's supposed to be me who's puking everywhere! Not
you.

PETE: Ha ha.

SHAWNA: Some of us puke.

Some of us shake.

I sweat.

If you kill a kid there's bound to be a reaction.

It happens.

PETE: I'm okay.

Really.

I'm okay.

RAMON: Drink?

PETE: Please.

He pours.

PETE: Thank you.

They drink.

A moment.

ALICE: You know what?

I'm glad the kid is dead.

…

I mean it.

…

I think we try too hard to stop kids being killed.

I think more kids should be killed.

I mean, why would we expect them to stop attacking us unless they believe we're more powerful than them. How can we expect them to believe we're more powerful than them if we constantly protect their kids?

That isn't what war is?

Is it?

War is killing kids.

It's not chivalry. It's not surgery. It's not mountain climbing.

Dead kids are not an unfortunate accident in war.

Dead kids are the point.

Aren't they?

That's what makes us not want it.

That's why we avoid – we surrender.

Any man can sacrifice himself. Any men can sacrifice his wife. But his kid? Nobody wants to see their kid torn up by a bomb, do they? Nobody wants to see their kid stuck on the end of a bayonet, do they? I mean it's simple human instinct.

So if you don't want someone to do something, you need to make them believe that if they do it, you'll kill their kid.

It's pretty simple.

They know it.

But we spend all our time avoiding that.

Is there any wonder this war's dragged on for a decade now? If we keep their kids alive?

Why are they even there, anyway.

These kids.

Why are they even in Waziristan?

Why don't they go somewhere else?

Why don't their parents emigrate?

If I was in Waziristan.

If I lived in a place where they throw acid in girls' faces. Where they live in huts. Where they drink from wells. I would leave.

Why don't they leave?

They have legs.

Whenever I try to imagine myself there, I get about as far as drawing water from a well and then and then I just think – fuck this. I mean fuck it. I'm outta here.

They live there because that's how they want their world to be.

They want their kids to be there.

That kid was being brought up by terrorists. He ran errands for terrorists, he brought tea to terrorists, passed notes for terrorists. He sat on the knees of terrorists. He brought emotional comfort to terrorists.

Terrorists loved that kid.

I'm glad he's dead.

I think his death will be a blow to them.

They will think harder next time they want to blow up Americans.

The rules of war. Those rules make me laugh. Do our enemies observe the rules of war. Of course not. Would we if we were in their shoes? If they were attacking us with drones would we refrain from carrying bombs into their malls? Would we refrain from attacking and raping their women? Would we refrain from spraying their primary schools with bullets?

What is a suicide bomb anyway but an improvised drone.

They unleash war upon us but we do not unleash war back upon them.

We quail.

We should torture.

We should kill without mercy.

More specifically – we should use the technological advantage we have to deliberately target children. There is no greater pain than to see your own child dead.

They will only stop when it hurts.

And killing children hurts.

I'm sorry.

Perhaps it's my hormones.

Perhaps it's carrying this little one that has brought clarity.

A moment.

Come on guys.

This is one of those days you see everything in perspective.

Look at us!

Good jobs. In a good town. Good friends. Good partners.

Good food!

Great country.

Warm night.

Warm friendship.

Warm white wine.

We're here now, we're alive and we're happy.

And there's a little one on the way.

It's been a big day for everyone.

But let's forget it now.

Let's move on.

ALICE pours wine for everyone.

ALICE: To the future.

To us.

To the kid.

To the kid?

Discomfort. No one drinks.

WWW.OBERONBOOKS.COM

Follow us on www.twitter.com/@oberonbooks
& www.facebook.com/OberonBooksLondon